Here's to a
successful business
& a happy family.

Jolene Brown

TO:

_____

FROM:

_____

Sometimes You Need More Than a 2x4!

ISBN 978-696-30079-0

Jolene Brown, CSP
www.JoleneBrown.com

Published by
Successful Farming® Custom Publishing
1716 Locust Street
Des Moines, IA 50309

Author: Jolene Brown
Designer: Matthew Eberhart
Art Director: Matt Strelecki
Editor: Cheryl Tevis
Copy Editor: Paula Barbour
Product Manager: Diana Willits

Photo on page 6 by Linda Behle; Photo on page 140 by SuperPhotoVideo.com;
Photo on page 136 by SuperPhotoVideo.com; All other photos Dreamstime.com.

Successful Farming Magazine
Publisher: Scott Mortimer
Editor-in-Chief: Loren Kruse
Vice President/Group Publisher: Tom Davis

Successfulfarmingbooks.com

Printed in the USA

Sometimes You Need More Than a 2x4!

How-to-tips to successfully grow a family business

by Jolene Brown

Foreword

I can't help it. My German genes require me to admire beautifully kept farmsteads with well-organized livestock facilities and materials handling centers pleasing to the mind and eye. But my in-box at Successful Farming magazine often portrays a less pretty, messier picture of the operation. Letters, emails and personal conversations with parents, grandparents, children and in-laws reveal a great amount of frustration, resentment and hurt feelings from some members of family farm businesses. They are seeking help and don't know where to turn.

I wish every one of them could know my friend Jolene Brown. Now, through *Sometimes You Need More Than a 2x4!*, they can. Jolene is a successful family farmer, a sought-after family business consultant, and a popular professional speaker. She tells you what you need to hear with spot-on humor and experience so that you will listen. She not only instructs but also inspires and impels people to action. In working with clients, she easily assumes the role of the conscience of the family business. More than that, she provides the needed guidance based on her experience. Her practical tips lead to the successful results desired by the family members and required by the family business to thrive for another generation.

Family farm businesses are precious and amazingly enduring. Despite a lot of talk of mega corporations entering production agriculture, family farms still produce 86% of all farm production by dollar value. As editor-in-chief of a magazine with "success" in the title I know that farm families measure success in many ways. I've observed, however, that families who professionally achieve their business goals first find it easier to meet other outcomes the family values, too. This book is for every farm family member who desires to harvest the benefits of a successful business-first family.

Loren Kruse
Editor-in-Chief
Successful Farming magazine

This isn't just any ol' farm. This is our farm.
It's been walked over, toiled over, cried over, rejoiced over.

Many years ago a Farmer Brown invited me to join him and this farm.
I said "Yes" and at that moment received the gift of a loving man,
and the gift of a working farm. I am blessed.

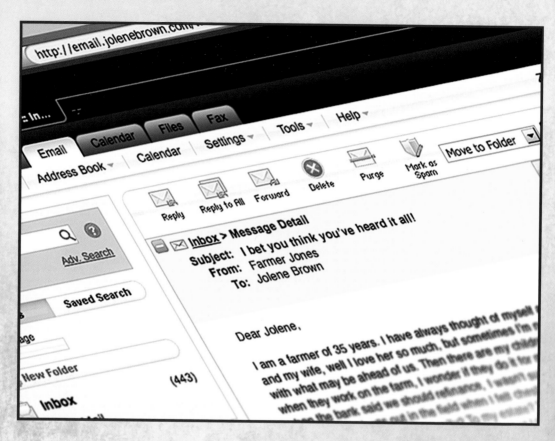

And so the multitude of stories and requests from those in family business begin. No, I haven't heard it all, but I have listened to, studied and learned a lot about working in a family business. It's time to share the lessons learned.

— *Jolene Brown*

Introduction

This is what I know.

After working with so many in family businesses - at their kitchen tables, family board rooms, or hotel meeting rooms - through late night phone calls and gut-wrenching e-mails - through boxes of tissues and stress-caused heart attacks … I have learned there is a major difference in the relationships and results of a Family-First Business and a Business-First Family.

In both situations, we have "genetics" working together…or trying to.

In a **Family-First Business**, decisions are most often based on emotions, feelings, personalities, genetics, wishes, avoidance, habits and assumptions. Sometimes those decisions work out well for everyone. (I call that good luck.) But the majority of times, it leads to problems…first within the family, then within the business. The results are often the saddest of heartbreaks, unfulfilled dreams, a breakdown of family relationships, or the loss of the business, the place they wanted to work happily together.

In a **Business-First Family**, decisions are based on an agreed mission, written goals, a code of conduct, discussions, clarifications, quality communication, legal and written documentation, and carefully managed risk. Then all become more respected and respectful, therefore more engaged, more productive, and more profitable. Then we have a happy family.

A successful Business-First Family does not sacrifice family for business, but values the family and has the family's best interest at heart…that's why they do the business correctly.

Throughout my 20+ years as a professional speaker and family business consultant, I've had the privilege to hold up a mirror to many a family business. As one strong, surprised and appreciative leader said, "I can't believe this. You've been on-site, working with us for two days and you already know more about our business than we do." I've had a mother call with laughter in her voice, thanking me as she explained her husband's befuddled response to her new assertive… "Stop! Sounds like you have a problem with Joe. I think you need to talk to him." Then she walked away!

She also said her stomach had stopped hurting because she no longer is the "dumping ground" for everyone in the family. I honored a young couple who knew it was time to leave a no-win family business situation, and found a retiring rancher eager and appreciative of their attitude and willingness to work. I've also helped family members discuss a multitude of reasons why they could not work together…and then recommended they not work together. But they could still be family.

These are not unique situations. When I finish my workshops, whether they are throughout the U.S. or countries beyond, attendees always give me a heart-felt thanks for the insight, laughter and take-home tools they've gained. They encourage me to continue to share with others because they know so many other family businesses in the same situation.

Isn't it ironic that in agriculture we're taught weeds, seeds, breeds and feeds, even cash flow and marketing…but we're not taught what to do with, or how to work with people – our most important resource?

What do we do when someone's not pulling his share? When silence, grunts, or assumptions are the communication default? Where work and self-worth are so intertwined we fear transition? Where entitlement clashes with work ethic and appreciation? When things go wrong – through no fault of our own?

This book addresses these and other common challenges I've encountered as I work with clients and members from groups such as The American Farm Bureau Federation®, the World Potato Congress, Royal Bank of Canada and many more.

As a spokesperson and champion of the family-owned business, I am able to reach and teach my audiences through my personal experiences as an Iowa farmer, the educational research I've done, and the lessons I've learned from clients. All have taught me essential keys to build a successful Business-First Family.

Many of the insights in this book will reaffirm that you are on the right business path and acting in ways that contribute to the quality of relationships you want with your family members. Some of these ideas may cause you to stop, think about what you're doing or haven't done, and decide there's still time for a better way.

Perhaps most importantly, I hope you'll share this book with your family business members and use it as a catalyst for conversation. Keep this book in your kitchen, on your desk, in the shop office or gathering place so you can refer to it when you're facing a challenge or need a pick-me-up. The blend of practical tips and gentle reminders might help you turn intentions into actions and reason into results.

Do you really want the legacy of your
family business to continue?

It doesn't matter if the next generation is ready…if the senior generation isn't.

It doesn't matter if the senior generation is ready if the next generation isn't.

Legacy making requires a keen commitment backed by an earned transition of labor, management, leadership and ownership over a pre-determined period.

Just because you want to…

Doesn't mean you get to.

Being part of a family business
is **not** a birthright!

College students often tell me,
"I'm going back to the farm
after graduation."

I smile and ask,
"Have you been invited?"

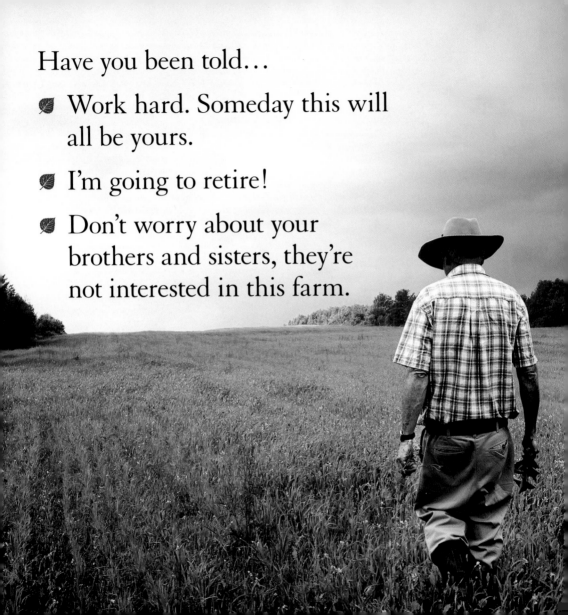

Have you been told…

- Work hard. Someday this will all be yours.

- I'm going to retire!

- Don't worry about your brothers and sisters, they're not interested in this farm.

Do not confuse a conversation
with a contract.

Words in a conversation sound good.

Words in a contract make sure
your word is good.

A distraught son shared,
"I always thought my father's word was
good enough. I was wrong."

Define "What" before "Who"

Choosing the best next leader for your business requires: first defining what characteristics and skills are needed to lead the business; then who is best qualified for that job.

If we don't do it this way, we often end up with the favored "golden child" and the business in a mess.

By the way, the best person to lead your business may or may not be a family member!

"How far you go in life depends
on your being tender with the young,
compassionate with the aged, sympathetic
with the striving and tolerant of the weak
and the strong. Because someday in your
life you will have been all of these."

— George Washington Carver

The farm or ranch won't take care
of you when you are sick or sad.

Your friends and family will.

What have you done to appreciate the important people in your world?

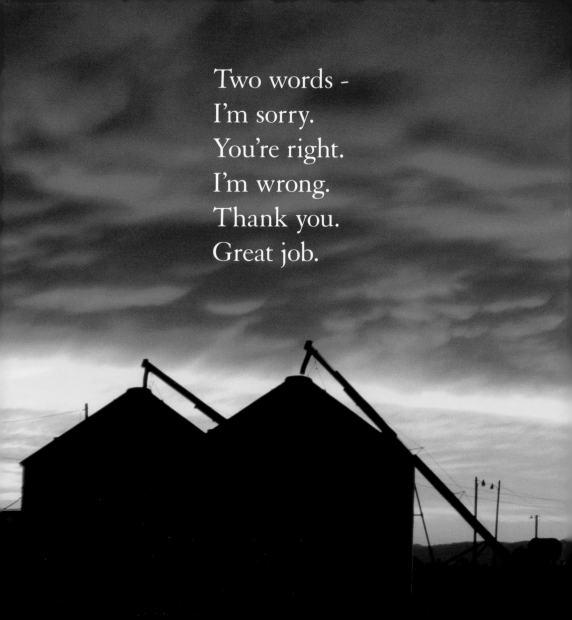

Two words -
I'm sorry.
You're right.
I'm wrong.
Thank you.
Great job.

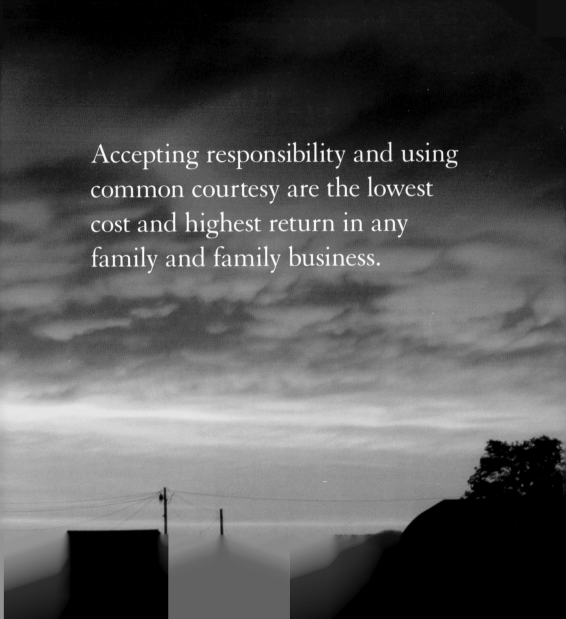

Accepting responsibility and using common courtesy are the lowest cost and highest return in any family and family business.

"Hire family members well because it's darn hard to fire them!"

— Jolene Brown, CSP

Before hiring, find out …

1. What talents and skills does this family member bring? Does the business need them or will it intentionally adapt to include?

2. Will the value justify the actual cost?

3. Has this family member worked 2 or more years for a non-family boss?

4. Does the family member demonstrate a maturity and capability to live independently of parents?

"A family business is not a place to rehabilitate a family member!"

— Jolene Brown, CSP

If there is someone in your family who is angry, addicted, arrogant or lazy, don't hire them.

No one else would.

Why should you?

Family members might offer guidance, ignore or even tolerate another family member's behavior, but a business must hire those whose conduct is aligned with a positive work team.

FAMILY EMPLOYMENT AGREEMENT

PROBATION:

"For the next 12 months, we have a probationary agreement. If at any time you, the employee, feel the business is not a good fit for you – or we, the hiring business, feel you are not a good fit, employment ends pending three weeks written notice – no hard feelings. We'll still be family but we will not work together."

Probation is important.

It grants mutual benefits for
all before you get locked in.

Worthy: having adequate or great merit, character, or value; meeting an important need; deserving of position; necessary.

Worthy applicants matched with worthy work make a better business and a happier family.

Use a business responsibilities chart to note who is in charge of each task.

Gradually transition management and leadership of tasks from one generation to another.

This builds confidence, and allows growth while the "wise master" is nearby to mentor.

The number one job of a leader
is to replace himself or herself.

What is your Total Compensation Package?

Family business members often regard their salary as a "meager" reward.

What have they forgotten? Fringe benefits!

Add up… housing, utilities, vehicle, fuel, health-dental-optical-life-disability insurance, retirement plan, fuel, edible groceries, phone plans, computer and more!

Shocking. So little is not so little.

PERSONAL

INSURANCE

FINANCING

Dental/Medical

BILLS

AUTOMOBILE

"We get paid so little!"

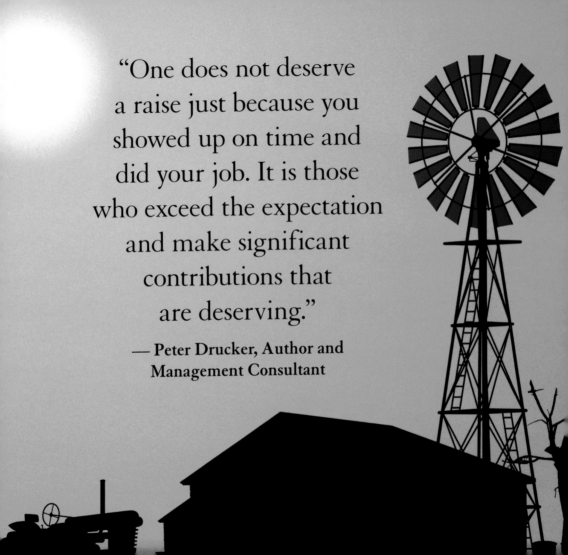

"One does not deserve a raise just because you showed up on time and did your job. It is those who exceed the expectation and make significant contributions that are deserving."

— Peter Drucker, Author and Management Consultant

Job descriptions tell you what to do and who is to do it.

Standards of the job tell you how well something needs to be done.

Those who go beyond the minimum, adding more value while helping others deserve recognition, reward and advancement.

A positive demonstration of attitudes,
behaviors and results happens before
any transition of assets.

"Be grateful for what you have in order to be worthy of what you want."

— Jolene Brown, CSP

All folks have a sense of humor…

It's just that some folks have a bad one.

"Hire the happy...They are
more fun to work with!"

— Kathy Brown, RN, CSP

Humor improves
morale, productivity,
problem solving,
rapport and loyalty.

Look in the mirror…

Would you hire yourself?

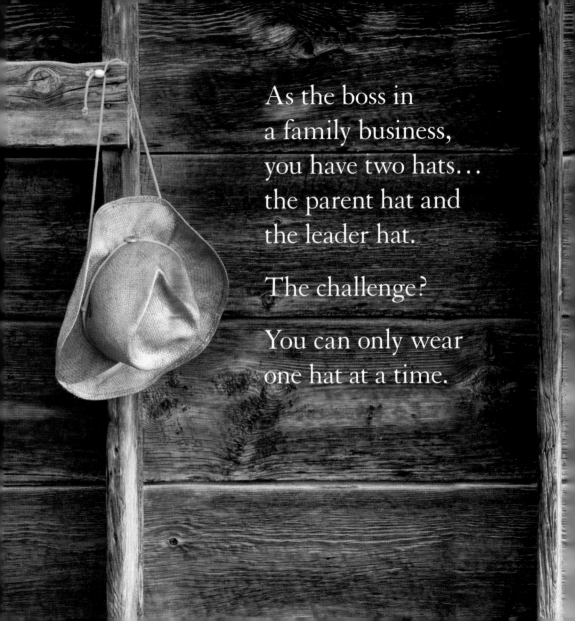

As the boss in a family business, you have two hats... the parent hat and the leader hat.

The challenge?

You can only wear one hat at a time.

EXAMPLE:

"I allowed my son's lack of performance to go on far too long. I finally told him he could no longer work here. He hasn't spoken to me since." — **Dad Hat**

"It was tough to fire a key employee, but even after coaching, he just wouldn't follow through on our agreed upon goals. The business deserves and demands a better performance." — **Leader Hat**

Talking about the same event…
two different hats.

"Why is it my parents can
still push all my hot buttons?

That's easy.

They installed them!"

— Coffee mug slogan

After my workshop, I'll not forget the tremor in one woman's voice nor her painful tears. "It's been a year since my husband died, and I'm still mad. Mad at him because he never explained things and left a real mess. Mad at myself for not asking questions."

Are you ignorant of important information? Don't think you need to know? Aren't included in the knowing?

Remember to share your important information with others. After all, leaving behind a mess can go both ways.

What details do you need to
know before it's too late to ask?

"Hope is not a good business strategy."

— Jolene Brown, CSP

HOPE RD

How much risk are you
willing to take in the hopes
things will be as you wish?

Surprises at the reading of a will
when an estate involves a family
business may be a catastrophe.

You have the legal right to distribute your estate as you wish.

But, if the estate assets affect business continuation, you need to let "the rules of the distribution game" be known.

Do this "early in the game" so all can prepare emotionally and financially for the future.

At death, everyone will have assets distributed – the state tells you how, or you can decide.

You'll like your choices better!

Pick up the phone and schedule a meeting with your advisors to formulate your plan and your will.

If your spouse won't go… go by yourself!

Habits, patterns and traditions
make for great family history.

Vision, creativity and commitment
make for a long-lasting business.

Part of your job is to be pleasant and polite!

A number of times I've shared with those in the workplace…

"You don't have to like it, you just get to do it. Now, if you happen to like it, the result is better for the both of us!"

A new daughter-in-law asked…

"How long do you have
to be married before you
get to be family?"

The business must decide, "What, if any, is the business role of a spouse?"

In-law family members must express their wishes, if any, for inclusion or involvement in the business. It's best clarified before a ring is on the finger.

Want to avoid frustration and problems among family co-workers?

Have each family unit own its own house.

You might lose a tax deduction, but sniping, jealousy and resentment often are the result when a family has no power to make independent decisions about its own home.

There are worse things
than paying taxes.

"Ignoring the obvious
isn't ignorance, it's stupidity."

— Audience member,
Beef Improvement Association, Australia

While consulting at a kitchen table, I asked an older couple about their will.

"We think we've got one somewhere."

After tracking it down in a back drawer, I noted a list of guardians.

"How old are your children?"

Mom's sheepish admission, "40 and 42."

If you have guardians listed for your children and they are well over the age of 18, chances are your will needs to be reviewed and revised!

Is it time to update your will?

A mom lamented that her husband had not come to the hospital to visit their 3 year old daughter with spinal meningitis.

I asked Dad for "his side of the story."

He replied, "I have to milk and besides, I've had my cows for 13 yrs, I've only had her for 3."

Smoke came out of my ears!!

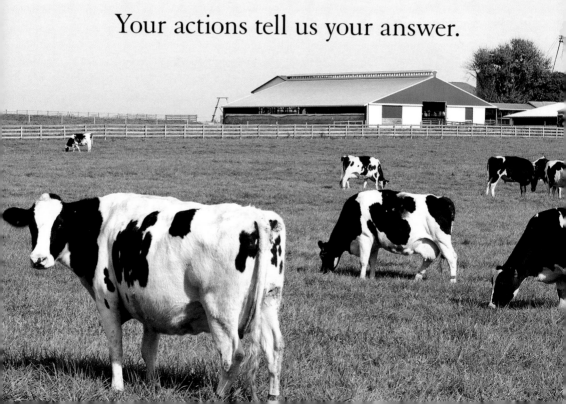

What's more important?

Your kids
Or
Your cows?

Your actions tell us your answer.

"Sometimes you just need a 2x4."

— Jolene Brown, CSP

"My gosh, woman. Use your head."

— Husband

"Sorry, I was using my heart."

— Wife

"We can't reason someone out of something they weren't reasoned into."

— Jonathan Swift

You won't believe what they did to us."

"You won't believe how we were treated."

These statements often are followed by
sad sagas of resigned defeat and decades of
dashed hopes.

Here's what I've learned. You can't
always control what has happened to you…
but you need to face reality and make
peace with your past so it won't mess
up your future.

You have learned important lessons of
how not to treat someone else.

When someone approaches me with a sad saga, I ask:

- 🍃 Has something unfair or undeserved happened to you?

- 🍃 Did you cause it?

- 🍃 Can you change it?

If not, write down the lesson learned, file it away and move on.

It's hard to be excited about today or plan the future if you carry the emotional weight of an unchangeable past.

What would happen if your succession
plans, or lack of them, took effect today?

A rancher was adamant about leaving his large estate equally to both of his children.

One son had been in and out of drug rehab 3 times, and was again using.

I wonder if a windfall for that son might create a different outcome than what Dad wanted.

Fair is not always equal.

LEGACY QUESTIONS

Do you really want this business to continue?

How would it function when you or your assets are not present? Will those in the business keep control?

Have those in the business received market value compensation or promises that sweat equity now will bring a reward later?

What's the net worth growth contributed by those working in the business?

Have you explored options with your advisors?

Ask an accountant and financial planner for help with a roadmap of:

- 🍃 your future financial needs;
- 🍃 business financial needs;
- 🍃 next generation financial needs.

It's only when each picture is clear that everyone sleeps better.

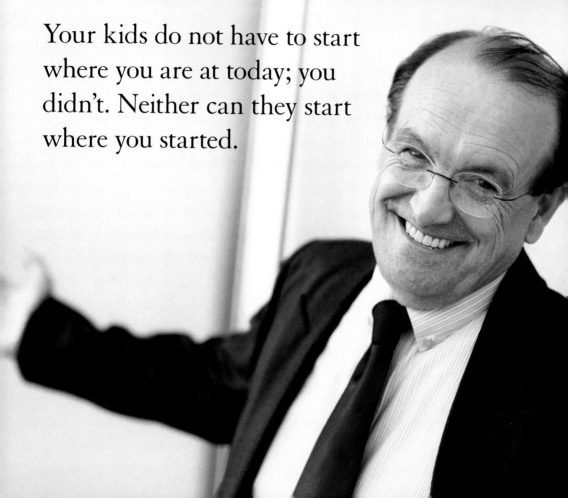

Senior generation, take care of yourself financially first.

Your kids do not have to start where you are at today; you didn't. Neither can they start where you started.

"It takes less time to do a thing right
than to explain why you did it wrong."

— Henry Wadsworth Longfellow

"The mark of a successful business isn't whether or not it has problems; it's whether it has the same problems it had last year."

— John Foster Dulles

When asked specific questions about the farm's finances, a rancher replied,

"I'll be glad to show you the books, but which set of books do you want to see? The one I have for the IRS, the one I show my advisor, or the one that's real?"

Oops.

To operate as a successful Business-First Family your one set of books must be transparent, timely, and accurate.

"You must have tools and use them while times are good so they'll be there when times get tough."

— Jolene Brown, CSP

Successful Business Tools

- Goals
- Business Plan
- Job Descriptions
- Compensation Package
- Code of Conduct
- Buy/Sell Agreement
- Meeting procedures
- And many more…….

Make sure your Buy/Sell Agreement or Exit Strategy is a separate document from your will.

You might have a clear expectation for transition of assets, only to learn that a will can be changed on a whim!

Don't know what to do?

Take this three-question ethics test.*

1. Is what I am about to do legal?

2. If my actions were to appear as the headlines in my local newspaper, would that be OK?

3. If my family and friends knew about my actions, would they cheer me on?

If your answers sit well in your gut and heart, you have a foundation to support your action.

*Adapted from The Power of Ethical Management, Kenneth Blanchard and Norman Vincent Peale

Do you have a written Code of Conduct for your family business team?

If so, you'll spend less time sitting on the fence and more time in aligned productivity.

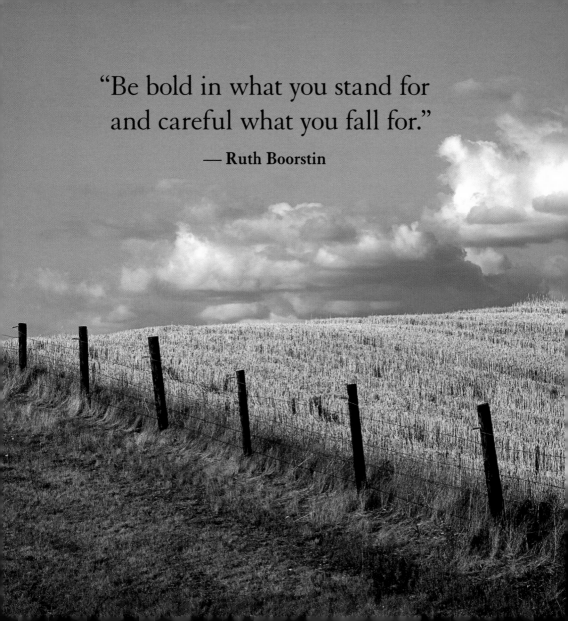

"Be bold in what you stand for and careful what you fall for."

— Ruth Boorstin

When your values are clear, decisions are easier.

"We don't go running away from our values. We go drifting away, and one day wake up in a place we never meant to be, drifting in a direction we would have never chosen."

— John Blumberg, CSP,
Author of Good to the Core

When seeking information or clarification about a problem, carefully choose your opening words.

Beginning with the word "Why?" sparks a defensive position. You're asking someone to prove it to you.

Start with phrases such as,

"Would you help me understand
the reasons for…"

"What would happen if…"

"Could we also…"

These phrases invite a conversation
and build a stronger team.

Hand signals…
Panels of switches…
"Go ahead, come back"…
Metric or standard…
"No, not that cow!"…

How am I supposed to know??

"Mind reading is not
an acceptable form
of communication!"

— Jolene Brown, CSP

Do you know the #1 thing a spouse wants from his or her partner in a family business?

Security.

How's yours?

If you want to keep "harmony" in the family business, honor your in-laws.

Once a month a wise mother-in-law takes her daughters-in-law to lunch. Nice place. Pays for child care and the meal. She asks about their world, work, friends, family. She listens. She cares. They learn and laugh and are graciously grateful for each other.

Is it time to schedule a "daughter-in-law" lunch?

One of the highest compliments you can give a member of your work team is honest praise in the presence of his or her spouse.

Then both can be deservedly proud of their hours of work.

Multiply Good News

"My parents always told me
I wouldn't amount to anything
because I procrastinated so much.
I told 'em, 'Just you wait.'"

— Judy Tenuta

Educating the next generation requires more than the old habit responses:

- watch and then you'll know;

- get out of my way, I can do it quicker;

- or read my mind.

Be patient and clear as you teach those less skilled or experienced. The best ideas just might come from them.

Are you
a coach
or a critic?

If you want someone
younger to someday
walk without you…

…it is best if you first give them a chance to walk beside you.

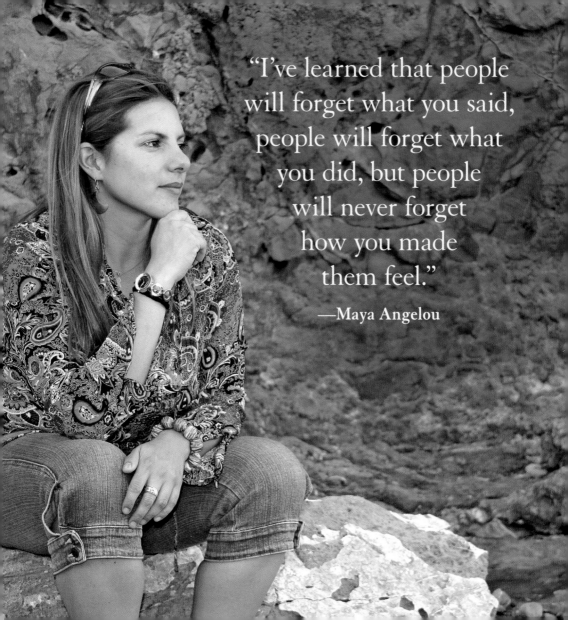

"I've learned that people will forget what you said, people will forget what you did, but people will never forget how you made them feel."

—Maya Angelou

Have you had good coaches in sports, music, 4-H, FFA? What made that coach "good"?

Write down those characteristics. Compare that list to your style as business coach to the next generation.

How are you doing?

If you don't like change, you're going to like obsolescence even less.

A rancher finally told me his real thoughts about bringing his daughter into the business.

He said…

"As long as she doesn't change anything, I'm flexible!"

Perhaps you've heard…

"If you always do what you've always done, you'll always get what you've always gotten."

I disagree.

You'll be out of business. The pace, people, process and products for agriculture have changed.

Have we?

"The next generation knows things we need to know, but may not want to learn."

— Jolene Brown, CSP

Don't retire.

Refire!

The word "retirement" leaves a bad taste in the mouths of many farmers and ranchers.

But, if you move from retirement to "refirement," there is excitement when the next opportunity is planned and in place!

With that attitude, you'll still be welcomed and needed as "the wise consultant".

People have to live until they die!

Plan ahead!

1. What are you going to live on?

2. How do you want to live?

3. Where is your security?

4. Have you met with your advisors and realistically explored your needs for retirement?

A farmer laments…"How am I supposed to have time to do all of this other stuff. The work is never done!"

And he was right…the work never is all done.

Instead of expressing this futility, say out loud…"The work will never all be done."

Sometimes just by saying, "The work will never all be done," you're also saying, "This is all I can do or need to do at this time."

This one simple exercise might lessen the "weight", allowing you to set a more realistic expectation, reduce stress, and celebrate all you have done.

Sometimes enough really is enough.

Plan, then take an annual vacation! The minute you put it on the business and home calendars, something good happens.

- ❧ You become more efficient because you have to be ready;

- ❧ Those around you increase efficiency because they know you'll not be there to work;

- ❧ Your family members light up with anticipation. They know you value them as much as your work.

Don't let your vocation become your vacation.

Keep your own humor journal!

This can be multiple spiral notebooks kept at your desk, the kitchen's pot-holder drawer, and the farm shop!

Write down funny things, joyful antics and words of children, a crazy cartoon or story…even dumb things you've done!

Why? When the going gets tough, that's when we most need the healthy benefits and perspective from humor!

"If you can laugh at it; you can live with it."

— **Erma Bombeck**

Blessed are we who laugh at
ourselves, for we shall never
cease to be amused!

DON'T FORGET

A successful Business-First Family does not sacrifice "family" for business. It values the family and has the family's best interest at heart...that's why they do the business correctly.

What have you done today to create or reinforce a respected, respectful, engaged, productive and profitable Business-First Family?

There is a huge difference between "saying" something and actually "doing" something.

Now is the time to do.

Eyes aglow. "How many acres, Daddy?"

Two little girls colored another segment on the large paper thermometer marking how many acres had been harvested each day.

They had already chosen the "When-We-Get-Done Celebration." They wanted to put on their fancy clothes and dance with mom and dad in the kitchen!

Day after day, anticipation built. "How many acres?"

Shoes polished. "How many acres?"

Dresses laid out! Finally, "How many acres?"

"WE'RE DONE! Let's dance, Daddy!!"

In his hurried, on-a-mission voice, Daddy replied… "Now the work really starts. I have to drain the oil, beat the weather for fall field work, winterize the…."

The little girls' eyes filled with tears.

Mom turned to Dad and said…"Are you sure you don't just have one hour to put on your fancy clothes and dance with your girls in the kitchen?"

They danced.

Have you really celebrated all you have done?

Perhaps it's time to dance in the kitchen!

Jolene is on a mission to share leading-edge best practices, appreciation, laughter and celebration with the people of agriculture. As an award-winning communicator, her professional speaking work is in demand as she teaches what it takes to increase productivity, profitability and peace of mind. She's a walking-talking spokesperson for agriculture and a champion for the family owned business.

As founder of the Business-First Family Institute™, she knows the unique challenges facing parents, siblings, and in-laws who work together every day. She lives the life of agriculture as co-owner and active partner on their Eastern Iowa corn and soybean farm.

And did we mention her sense of humor? Jolene believes if we aren't laughing, we're not learning. Her proudest accomplishment is when audience members come up to tell their story and say "I've never laughed so hard and learned so much." Evaluations often say "You know exactly what I'm going through." "Time flew by." "Dynamic." "Only session I didn't have to force myself to stay awake."

Her favorite? "I've heard Jolene many times and she is always excellent. Please have her speak again."

As a professional speaker, her audiences have been world-wide, diverse, deserving and demanding. With a unique blend of psychology, business, plain-speaking and down-home humor, her messages exceed expectations.

Jolene is a real "Farmer Brown." She knows what it's like to harvest from sun up to long after sun down. She knows what it's like to gather neighbors in her home when the electricity goes out in their rural area. She knows what it's like to bet a year's income on local and global weather, international markets, and political influences.

Most importantly, Jolene cares deeply about the ag industry. She's a passionate supporter and promoter of farm families and has developed a variety of programs and products that identify the challenges they face and steps they can take to maximize performance, productivity, profits ... and peace of mind.

Want to have Jolene speak at your upcoming events?

From fun-filled or theme setting keynotes, to eye-opening and value-packed general sessions, from moderating panels or "show and tell" to summarizing conclusions with "keepers and questions", Jolene will provide much more than the usual speaker. She often presents multiple times at a conference, and is asked back year after year!

Jolene is one of very few women worldwide to earn the designation of the Certified Speaking Professional (CSP). Planners attest to how easy it is to work with her, how she customizes content, how she is the go-to speaker for consistently high performance! The following are just a few of the hundreds of testimonials Jolene has received from satisfied program coordinators and meeting planners over the years. They depend on her experienced ability and adaptability to provide great value while leaving everyone uplifted, laughing and wanting more.

Jolene wants to hear from you!

She'd like to hear your family business stories, what drives you nuts, and what adds to your success. Who knows? You just might have the answer to someone's family business frustration, or share an idea to prevent a problem.

On her web site, www.JoleneBrown.com, you'll find her popular Six CD Album, "The Top Ten Stupid Things Families Do to Break Up Their Business!"™ As a farmer from Ontario, Canada shared, "How do you put a price on saving a family and improving a business? You can't, but the content from this album did both! Thanks, Jolene!"

Contact Jolene!

She's only a phone call or E-mail away!
Telephone (319) 643-2429 or email: Jolene@JoleneBrown.com

Follow Jolene!

Want to order volume copies for your group or event?
This book is available at discounts that make it realistic
to provide it as a gift for your customers and clients.

"Enlightening and entertaining."
— **Chester O. McCorkle, Director Northwest Agribusiness Executive Seminar,
Washington State University**

"Not only do you draw them in, you keep them there for the entire time and wanting
more afterwards. They were still swarming you after the closing session."
— **Regina Cleary, Commodity Classic**

"Every single evaluation form rated your presentation as "Excellent."
Comments included, "Best speaker I have ever heard." "We learned so
much we will be able to take back to our operations and families."
— **Cathy Day, Director of Special Programs,
Nebraska Farm Bureau Federation**

"Resolve of steel and heart of gold. Jolene Brown is fiercely committed to the
success of your Business-First Family. Jolene honed her skills consulting with farm
families across kitchen and boardroom tables around the world. Value her insights.
Heed her advice. You just might be able to put that 2x4 back in the barn!"
— **Patricia Katz, Productivity & Balance Strategist**